About the Author

Born in Stamford, Lincolnshire in the 70s, M.J Goodman has moved around in the UK and lived abroad with her service family. Finally in her twenties, she put down roots in Gloucestershire where she started her writing career as an absorbing hobby. She lives in Gloucester with her husband Peter.

Dedication

For my family – without whose love and support this dream
would never have been realised…

M J Goodman

MESSAGES FROM THE SOUL

AUSTIN MACAULEY PUBLISHERS™

LONDON • CAMBRIDGE • NEW YORK • SHARJAH

A CIP catalogue record for this title is available from the British Library.

ISBN 978-1-7869-3938-8 (Paperback)
ISBN 978-1-78693-939-5 (Hardback)
ISBN 978-1-78693-9401- (E-Book)
www.austinmacauley.com

First Published (2017)
Austin Macauley Publishers Ltd.
25 Canada Square
Canary Wharf
London
E14 5LQ

Acknowledgements

I'd like to thank everyone at Austin Macauley first of all, for their input, advice and guidance, also for deciding to publish my book in the first place.

I'd like to thank my friend Jan G, who first suggested I express my feelings through the written word.

Thanks to my many friends on social media for allowing me to indulge myself by writing poems about them, their life situations and their beloved pets and also for bolstering my confidence with their enjoyment of my daft scribblings – too numerous to mention here but you all know who you are! Thanks to posse pals for providing laughs along the way – again you know who you are. Thanks to KM and Pete my husband for listening to my work and finally persuading me to submit my poems to a publisher.

Next I would like to thank my parents for their helpful comments, constructive criticism and also their continuing interest, sincere amusement and loving support for me in this new adventure as it unfolds.

Finally, last but most importantly, my undying love thanks and gratitude goes to my husband Peter – Pete – my rock. This is for his patience and tolerance while I hide myself away at the computer, proof reading, editing and composing new poems. Also for his genius comic wit and ability to supply me with a series of inspired (and inspiring) titles such as "Rabbit Pie" and "The Written Word Unwritten" amongst others. And finally for his staunch support, love, exceptionally hard work and frequently voiced confidence in my ability as a writer of verse. Darling – I couldn't have done it without you!

Blood Lust

There's a tapping at the window
Now a knocking at the door
A handsome stranger in the night time
Who leaves no shadow on the floor

His wings flap in the twilight
As the moon begins to shine
The owls flee from the shadows
When the handsome cloaked acquaintance comes to
  dine

I don't know what you see in him
He exudes a tainted vibe
I only want your happiness
I don't trust at what he connives

Again I come to see you
But you are not really here
And still inclined to trust him
Though he draws your senses far elsewhere

He uses no horse or carriage to journey to your door
And although his garb is richly woven
I've seen him sneer − look down on the poor
Don't trust him please don't trust him I fear his past
  is mired in gore

Why visits he only at night

When the blessed sun is gone
It seems to me he only comes in dusken times
When the devil's work is done

Last eve I saw you unexpectedly
In his lustful arms a passionate clinch
When his mouth moved to your neck
I noticed you did not even flinch

The thrall that he has you in
I do not deign to understand
But I fear for you my darling
Whilst he has pretensions to your hand

This morning you said you felt unwell
Your face was moonlight pale
However I fear this is no common disease
The one from which you ail

You wrap yourself in cloaks and scarves
To shelter from the cold
But the dual angry wounds upon your throat
Tell of evil as even I foretold

You are fading before my very eyes
Shrinking from the light of day
Your vampire lover's days are marked
I vow that I will make him pay

Damn you Sir God damn you
For turning my beloved lady's head
My once fairest of all maidens
Has become one of the feared undead

Her love is now shut off from me
Monsignor Drake he locked that door
But the thought that my love I must destroy
Cuts me to my very core

Now as I stand beside her bed
And on her beauteous face I gaze
I know that I have to make an end
And my eyes with tortured tears gaze

She who once was perfect as a summer's day
Has now become a hollow shell
A bloodless soulless vessel
Whose spirit I must send to hell

As the stake entered her body
Her eyes opened full wide
The whites bloodied and jaundiced
Like a true demonic bride

As the spike invaded further
Her unearthly screams rent the air
Increasing my unleavened grief
Guilt and heartbroken despair

At last the deed is done
My own dear love is dead and gone
As she exhaled her final breath
The pain to me was like living death

Alack and alas I am truly undone
Oh that I had been more watchful

After my poor love's spirit was gone
A bat flew in through the window
with me in no state to run

I was too late to save her
So had to make an end
And because of my own foolishness
I can make no amends

For the creature who then entered
Was not of mortal form
'Twas my nemesis Nosferatu
Come my future to transform

You stole my eternal lover
The vile monster hissed
For that I'll plague you for eternity
As his fangs punctured my wrist

So now I roam the nights alone
Far from all those that I love
For how can I dare go near them
When what I crave is human blood

I skulk deep in the darkest shadows
An exile from the light
I share this loneliest existence
With the creatures of the night

The moral of this bitter tale
Is now plain for all to see
If you consort with vampires
You will rue your destiny.

He's Gone

At last he's gone
After months of indignity, years of brave borne pain
He's gone to where there are no fears
No one to lay him claim.

Well his spirit has gone away, but what is left behind?
His grieving wife of many years is now on her own again

His family searching very hard for comfort
Where there is yet none for them to find.
He was a man of principles of morals sound and true
A faith that might make others quail

But stood him in good stead for the harsh trials of Life's
    battlefield
Which lay not too far ahead.

He's gone, he's gone, it's over the ups and downs of health
The lingering damaging destructive run of a cruel disease
    untamed and unbound that confined him, robbed him of life's
    wealth.

He's gone – All is gone
Death – the old and sick man's friend
Has taken all that pain away
Which no physician could hope to mend.

He's gone to pastures new and pure

Where there are no threats or pain
And before time has passed too far
He'll greet family who have gone before.

He's gone, he's left – his time is done
Sadly there can be no return
All that remains a family's grief
Building to a slow burn.

Hope

I was lost far out at sea
Without a dream of rescue
The beasts of terror beneath the waves
Held many fears for me

The drowning feelings of my mind
Left no room for more
The writhing depths – their currents strong
I always will abhor

For out to me you stretched a hand
No thought for your own soul
The burning brand in that dark night
Could help my wounds resolve

The tortures that I suffered
Whilst in the maelstrom
They are no more so painful
You helped me brave the storm

Although the clouds still glower
Above the battling seas
These waters hold less fear for me
You responded in my hour of need
you answered all my pleas

These days those fearsome seas are calm
The sun warms crystal bays

Thanks to you the future's clear
And I am on my way

You are the catalyst called Hope
A beacon in the dark
You help strangers to find the way
Helped me to find the path.

I Travelled with The Stars Last Night....

I travelled with the stars last night
Each one a sparkling dream
Each one a beloved child's soul
Whom Earth would never see

They lingered not in our green fields
too precious to remain
rising swiftly to the sky
with starlight's glint and flame.

Each star child they spoke to me
"we have no pain or fear;
never grieve or pine for us,
We see your every tear"

"Whenever you are lonely;
things don't seem right or clear
lift your eyes up to the sky
and know we love you dear"

"Though we rest beyond your sight
we fill the skies with life
therefore we know you won't forget
the heavens ease our strife"

Then I met a special star – glimmering and new
Her name – Phoebe Susan Grace – up in the sky so
  blue

she bid me pass this message –
Though she bides up on high insubstantial as a kiss
Her love for you; her dreams for you
Should fill you now with bliss

She never left you really to ascend to God above
Because she touched you dearly
Her heart so full of love.
She never left you truly
Though she appears just like a dream
Because you see her nightly
Her soft and gentle gleam

Though little Phoebe cannot appear again
in this world's mossy vales
She chases round the wind and rain
in comets' fiery trails

She bids you "Love"
She bids you "Live"
Enjoy life to the full
Because she's safe she has no pain
and she can fear no ill

Baby Phoebe and all her friends
Cherish and keep you warm
Because you deeply care for them
then they will know no harm

I travelled with the stars last night
Not through a telescope's embrace
The brightest star amongst them all...?
A little girl named Phoebe Susan Grace.

Longing for Release

The telephone keeps ringing
In the echoes of my mind
Though in my heart still searching
For voices too long quiet to find

They used to speak so clearly
Though now they seem to hide
Oh; how I long to know them
But that I am denied

I never stilled their voices
Though they still come around
I see them voice thoughts plainly
But the very noise is drowned

The shout of cheer, the laugh of joy
Are cut off to me now
For nature she has turned on me
And turned the volume down

I yearn to be at one with all
Though that will never be
That unseen power is gone for good
Can be no more for me

They never gave a signal
No glaring beacon fire
To let me know; prepare myself

For the loneliness that could not expire

So if you were to ever choose
To lose the sense of hearing
Then please I beg pass it to me
To love before death comes nearer

I would not grieve the loss of sense of place
Or even fear of dying
But please to grant me the gift of welcome sound
That sends my spirit flying.

Midnight Storm

Twilit dusk is long past now
Though still some hours 'til morn
Who knows what damage could be wrought
Before the blushing dawn

The stars won't linger long tonight
As storm clouds start to gather
Clashing close with all their might
They rend the sky asunder

As midnight looms the torrents pour
Hungry to devour the naked ground
All twisting round a boiling shower
The thunder cracks and branches snap
Through Nature's frenzied power.

The brooding banks of this storm front
Have not yet spent their anger
Barns are wrecked gates ripped from posts
No one is safe from danger

The skies loom dark still darker now
Storm demons not appeased
By evil mayhem wrought below
Tempests o'er the seas

As the crested horses rush the shore

The light house keeper hunkers down
The angry currents build again
The sea bed erupts still more

The broken crust of Earth's own skin
Spews lava in its anger
A new land will be born quite soon
All from the typhoon's hunger

No part of this world is safe tonight;
No part will remain unravaged
All mortals who on earth do roam
May be by nature savaged

For Nature knows no master
She brooks no show of power or will
When she unleashes fury
The world will feel it ill

The storms at midnight are the worst
It is darkest before the dawn
Mother Nature stands not still
But lets the earth be torn

But though the earth be torn apart
And though the seas know no surcease
Eventually all will be calm
Blanketed in peace.

Rabbit Pie

Bunnies, rabbits, conies
Hopping across the grass
Dreaming of lettuce and carrots
Coming from the pass

Noses twitching, ears alert
They go about their lives
Eating, mating, sleeping
Families; young ones, husbands, wives

The babies gambol happily
Amidst the buttercups
Flashing their little snow white scuts
Living life on the up

They comb their ears and crop the grass
They clean their bedrooms out
They relax beneath the sun's warm rays
When that glorious orb is out

They wrinkle their noses at dew
They flash their tails at will
They have fun, play in the sun
And when the day ends the play is done

At dusk a different beast appears
One that is full of fear
The night is full of dangers

And a rabbit is no seer

The woods become a feeding ground
The roads a killing zone
For hungry meat-eating wildlife
And humans who still roam

A rabbit in the headlights
is one without a hope
A rabbit in front of the hunter's gun
Should escape down the   nearest slope

But the rabbit caught in the poacher's trap
Is destined sure to die
The best that it can hope for
Is to taste good in Rabbit Pie.

Remarks to A Grieving Soul

The stinging hot tears of anger, of grief and of remorse
The feeling of desperate hopelessness – no access to recourse
I f you could turn such things around
The whole world has no doubt you would

But sometimes though you feel that way
Nature can be callously cruel
Although you try to make those turns
Disease can very swiftly overrule

You should not blame or hate yourself
It is no fault of aught
Just be kind to yourself and others
The ones who long to hold you close

Do not be afraid to down the walls
To show them how you feel
All they want to do is love
Help you, get you to heal

For time is no great healer,
it will not ease the pain
it just provides some detours
to help knit the damaged vein

So should you need to hold a hand
There's no need to feel shame
Just reach out and make your feelings known

You need never take the blame

Even though Death has its sad place
Life is destined to go on
There is still love here for you
To reinforce and make you strong

So do not hide, don't run away
Live in the here and now
We are all here to help
So step forward tall and proud.

Stormwinds

The clouds of night are gathering
Hiding the palest moon
Soon the winds will thrash their way
Way past the tattered dawn

The trees bear no defences
Against the heavens' impassioned rant
The gales won't cease to rend them
'Til Nature has her fury spent

The rain it rapes the ravaged land
The winds brook no reprieve
Nothing exists betwixt sky and earth
To calm this tempest's rage

The lightning rips the sky apart
Thunder devours my peace
Squalls and gusts tear at the ground
My heart beneath my feet

Who knows how long this ire will last
Not I though I'll still endure
Because the skies will lighten up again
'Ere you hail me from the shore

It is for you and you alone
The storm tossed waves I ride
Because you assuage my loneliness
By returning to my side.

Xxx The Art of Love – A Woman's Wish Xxx

The art of love is subtle
For gentleness a starring role
Passion also plays a part
The flame that sears the soul

My zest for life is strong
My need for love livelong
The need for love should never die
E'en when other emotions throng

I long for the thrill of foreplay
Anticipation of what's to come
The massage, stroking, tickling
That make my senses thrum

I need the stimulation of your touch
On silken flesh external
Before you venture further
Re-light the fires eternal

Intimacy; a simple jest
To enliven the emotions
It works so much more effectively
Than tonics, pills or potions.

I hunger for your sensual mouth
Lingering on mine
The pressure of your lips on me

Are akin to the divine

If you want to send me over the edge
Right up to heaven above
Then just practise these tender tricks
Skills in the Art of Love.

The Ba*tard

Nasty, griping, crushing, jibing
Tearing down your soul
The shredding of a character
Seems to be the bully's goal

He gets your senses wakened
Brings you to the ground
When all your emotions are flooded
He throws you in to drown

If you fail to founder
He'll find a way to breach
To wrench down your defences
Until hope is out of reach

He'll annihilate your sense of self
And swallow all your pride
Your joie de vivre he'll crush to death
To lie beneath your feet

But you cannot let him win this
For lo his time will come
When some strong soul will turn on him
And give him pause in time

For all bullies are cowards
That much is plain to see
And should never prove a threat

To either you or me

What goes around will come around
Bullies never prosper long
All that needs be done
Is for them to be shown they're wrong

Stand firm, be tough
Show you don't care
He won't know what to do
And before too long a time
He will no more be there.

The Clouded Mind

Have you ever known the torpor?
Of a clouded mind
A cloying smothering tumult
That seethes – is never left behind

The knowledge of confusion
The feelings of despair
A mind so densely clouded
Else empty as the air

No one can know that torment
Unless they have been there
The constant untethered maelstrom
That undermines the conscious mind

The clouds that gather boil and burn
Are a never-ending storm
Of thoughts that frighten numb and awe
In ever changing form

The teeming schemes
The thronging hells
Don't dissipate with ease
They continue in their whirling race
Without mercy or surcease

They linger never far away
Unless a kindly soul

Can help release the tortured pain
That simmers down below

A clouded mind from whence
The thunderheads have receded
Becomes a mind that's free again
To live to breathe to fly
But not with wings broken by fear
With those of angels up on high.

The Crucible of Shame

As I sat beside the hearth last night
Gazing into the flame
I glimpsed the fire sprites dancing
Caressing the kindling frame

I watched the sparks go flying
As they whirled in their frenzied heat
Biting at the tinder
Nestled in its stony bed

As I saw this happening
A furnace in miniature
It brought to mind the inferno
The Devil's domain beneath

Down underneath the surface
The sulphur and brimstone bubble; vats of liquid flame
Ready for those sinners
for whom Earth's evils were to blame

For evildoers and malfeasants
There is no escape from searing pain
While Hades' imps and demons
Continue to tend the crucible of shame

These imps and demons play their parts
They know their roles full well
For they once practised vice on earth

Such evil tales they could tell
They cheated friends, they defrauded folk
Never taking any blame
And after aeons – a milliard years
They nurse the crucible of shame

The sorry truth 'tis sad to say
The cauldron will never burn out
Evil will never quit the earth
Despite fair Justice' clout

So do yourself a favour
Acquit yourself of blame
Never be unrepentant sinning
And tied to the Crucible of Shame

Its contents will consume you
Bitter bile, acid, gall
Your soul would never be the same
Surrounded by the smoking pall

So would you dare the Devil's snare?
Never to return
To end up in a fiery bed
And never cease to burn

For me I prefer a fairer scent
Without the taint of evil
Which is why I disdain the Shaitan path
And spurn Hades and the Devil

I choose to walk the angel's way
Bathed in gentle pure white light

Not feel the burn and sting of hell
Evading eternal fiery night.

The Crumbling Towers

When strangers walk down English streets
I wonder what they might feel
The peace of cosy villages
With church altars where they could kneel

Do they feel comfort and security
Free from filth and grime
Or do they feel wrought with fear
Flinching as police car klaxons chime

Our land isn't the way it used to be
Our youth seem to know no shame
If people's homes are rendered no longer sacrosanct
They will never take the blame

These children know no boundaries
They have never seen the pain
They cause by all their fecklessness
While their curses fall like rain

The parents show them all the way
By example – or not being there
They lead them into evil traits
While good people can but stand and stare

But this is not in back street slums
This is in our very towns
The young they run like rabid dogs

While the legal system drowns

The people in their ivory towers
Are no longer in control
While the streets are full of looting thugs
With the hunger and greed of rage

They say that no one listens
That none of it is their fault
They think they are owed a favour
While they take England by the throat

The chieftains in their hallowed halls
Look on in desperate dismay
Little dreaming they may have helped
Contributed to the cause of this disarray

If they had gone another way
Been tougher from the start
Then mayhap we'd not be where we are
With our country torn apart

Plenty of our youth
Choose not to waste their time
They practise sports or play with cars
Or go off and rebuild the past

The other ones who don't comply
We need some other source
Of interest and occupation
To make their days go by

They need to be taught to respect

Both people and their place
They need to be shown how not to hate
Those of another race

They should not be put to one side
They should be put to work
Give them a sense of honour and purpose
That they will not want to shirk

So to stop the towers crumbling
Till they are no more to be found
Bring back National Service
For the idlers on the ground.

The Evil Gem

All who touch her feel the taint
The treachery, disdain.
This hardened soul, this poisoned gem
No holds bar her causing pain

She tears you up
Then drags you down
To the smallest size
Then after you have had far too much
She scorches you with her lies

Of enemies she has not few
She has her many spies
Should she be accused of foulest crimes
All truths she will deny
For her venom knows no curb
The gemstone –poison pearl

She dresses like a willing whore
With jewels and furs galore
She spends her days in luxury
No pauper at her core

If I could crush that oyster
With it's sickening treasure trove
I would destroy it through and through
Steel hand in velvet glove

However I need to leave that joy
For others to take on
I must go upon my way
Time for me to move on

I know that at the bitter end
Hot tears she will shed
For what she has done – She has to pay
Right will triumph in the end.

The Lake Siren

I walked down to the lake one day
And there a maiden saw
She seemed to float above the dew
A zephyr in the air

Her gown was flowing – blues and greens
Soft as a summer cloud
Her gentle gaze clear and serene
Her stature tall and proud

She danced upon the waters
Her face alight with joy
Her hair flows like river currents
In torrents and waterfalls

Her laughter sounds like azure streams
Trickling betwixt the rocks
Her voice the calm of ocean depths
That I could never see

I envy her that freedom
To linger in the waves
To commune in the freshet current
With nymphs and fish so free

For she has beauty pure and true
She knows no pain or fear
She has her friends around her still
Poseidon's landlocked seer

She beckoned to me join her
To sink beneath the watery sill
To see the aquatic wonders
Which overcame me with their thrill

I saw great forests of shimmering weed
Adorned with great jewels a-glistening
Great towers of bedrock they met my eyes
The palace of her fathers

She drew me further, further down
Into her peaceful domain
And although there dwell frightful storms
They never see kind rain

A myriad of beasts I saw
In those watery depths
Flocks of horses of the sea
And manatees all grey

And further of just within sight
I glimpsed their herders clear
Pale mermaids and fierce mermen

Their eyes as clear as air

They guarded their flocks with jealous pride
Never losing e'en a one
Even as the wind of currents glide
Through each maelstrom formed dell

Then came the time for my return
To the lands above
Thus I left the Goddess' home
Filled with thoughts of love

I never saw her beyond that day
Or aught else for that matter
For that day was the day I drowned
With no more dreams to shatter.

The Last Vigil

In the last watches of the night
The gathered surround the quiet bedside
Where a loved one lies his breathing slow
For this is the last vigil

A murmured question, a gentle sigh
But peace for all is not here yet
No one can tell when the time will arrive
As this is the last vigil

The man who lies there swathed in pale sheets
Is not aware of their presence at his head and feet
But they are aware and they watch him still
As he lingers and labours during this last vigil

His family surround him anxiously watchful
Knowing that pain is no longer an issue
Sometime far too soon his fight will be over
The vigil will not see the whole night through

They don't want to lose him – he doesn't want to go
At times restlessness shakes him fills loved ones with woe
He murmurs and twitches his breath fits and starts
This ended vigil will leave a big hole in several hearts

No rest for the watchers not yet a while
They cannot leave the bedside miss this travail
It's been a long time coming this glimpse of the end

But the vigil can only assist wounded hearts to mend

The atmosphere changes in the dim room
His breath has quickened and slowed and paused for a time
The pallor is gaining on his poor tired flesh
The vigilant reaper is nearby awaiting the thresh

He separates the soul from its vessel
The wheat from the chaff
But in sickness extreme this deed is a gift
Though those present will suffer when the soul is cast adrift

The silence has deepened – the darkness profound
For he is departed – one last breath resounds
The waiting is over the tears can now flow
For none can yet follow where he must go

A good life was lived a good man was loved
His passing will be remembered his being even more
For he was a hero, a good man and true
So here ends the vigil the last one he knew.

The Loss of Freedom

She mourned the loss of freedom
Born of toss of coin
Putting nails in the coffin
Of hope of fruiting loin

The demon lives within her
That robs her of this hope
Though it could one day destroy her
She has already learned to cope

The way it makes her feel
Effects on her daily life
They have no major impact
For she is full of fight

For this girl is very lucky
She has decades of life
Others do not fare so well
And only face sore strife

This freedom lost
Means not that much
Because she has a chance
A true chance of life of normal length
And not an early grave

Others are not so greatly blessed
They leave the earth too young

Through cancer; crash or crisis
Deserved life songs remain unsung

She prays for them
That they have peace
Because they have no pain
She joins the angelic chorus in its glorious refrain

No soul deserves ill-fortune
Through no fault of their own
For humans are born equal
'Tis in youth the seed of evil sown

Humans bear cruelty to their country
Yea some even to their blessed own
They may one day enshrine the earth
In evil's deadly shroud

But that is no sure reason
To fall back in the chase
To battle; sickness ill and suffering
Whilst in the Human race.

The moon came down
and whispered...

The moon came down and whispered
Not many eves ago;
He revealed me untold secrets
That no one else could know.

He narrated me a history
Of people whom I cherish;
These two have not known life too long
Their love constant will never perish
Despite the troubles they have known
Their future hopes stand strong.

These young ones of whom the lucent one spoke
Are abroad in foreign climes
Although moved far from closest kin
Will never be alone.

The pride of a younger country;
Far across the ocean deep
Ere a few years the woes they've felt
Have tested them in grief.
They knew not what the cause was
Of this very personal woe
The kindly moon vouchsafed it me;
Mother Nature was their foe
She robbed them of what they wanted most
And caused it to be lost.

The future for them is rosy now
The growth of a tiny seed
Has prospered and continued
To assuage a precious need.

The couples yearned for treasure
Now here for all to see
Will fuel their endless pleasure
Add years of mystery
That he has been so longed for
Completes youth's reverie.

This little soul; this little dove
For that is who he is
Has a name picked long before
Alexander Nathaniel Coulombe

May he know that he is loved;
Loved adored and cherished
And that as he travels the lifelong days
His parents love will never vanish.

The Road Less Travelled

Have you seen the road less travelled
It's not too far away
For you to take a chance
Traversing along that way

The journey could be easy
Or even full of joy
It might cause you pure terror
Or worries unalloyed

Though the path ahead is clouded
And you never can be sure
Just how it could all pan out
Please do not let that deter

The bravest souls will prosper
Even though they fear the worst
For they have pushed their boundaries
And yet have stayed the course
Even if those around you;
can offer no support
do not turn away that chance
to wander in foreign courts

Only you can change your future
It's just a short distance away
Go; take the road less travelled
And live your dreams some day.

The Shifting Sands of Home

The wind assails the Spring warm trees
In gardens of the realm
Yet these can never ever compare
To the shifting sands of home

Oh how I yearn to feel the heat
The burn of desert sun
The glint of mica on dune's side
Since life had e'er begun

I dream of isles in regions tropic
Not distant from that place
Where I can be at peace
And not walk where others deign to roam

I long to see those crystal dunes
To hear the siren winds
To tread the tracks so rarely trod
Of that place I left behind

That place I left so long ago
It is there still untouched
At night the stars caress it still
Those sands that I so love

The beach on which I linger now
The treasures for which I comb
For me they keep no secrets

Like the shifting sands of home

The whispers from there haunt me still
Sometimes the pain's too much
The dreams where I can hear, taste, see
Can feel but never touch

The shifting sands are calling now
Not from some dusty tome
But from my own country beneath the sun
The shifting sands of home.

The Spirit of Light

The light streams through my window
Dissolving all the pain
Easing the discomfort
So oft brought on by rain

I mourn the loss of summer
The turn to gloomy night
The shortening of dearest daylight
Which brought me pure joy unconfined

I long for days resplendent out in the golden rays
They fill me up
They calm me down
Those balmy radiant days

These days of gold stray far away
Though glow still in my heart
For I know that they must come again
Though now so far apart

I wile away autumnal wintry months
Immured against the dark
Curled in a bright cocoon of my love
Not fearing the black hound's bark

The black dog will not linger here
He has other souls to meet
He visits me but rarely now

Your light washes o'er my feet

The light within me shines right out
It stands me in good stead
To live and love until the sun returns
From his dark wintry bed

He will return I know that now
I was not always so sure
But with your love to succour me
I mourn his loss no more.

The Strait and Narrow Way

I have walked a road of pain; times past
It seemed to have no end
No remission from the grief
Nor any who could defend

That road of pain it taught me
That solutions don't spring up
They take some time to search for
It said "never give up"

The little roadside altar
The diptych icon there
The blackbird in the hedgerow
Made it easier to bear

The stars high in the gloaming
The reeds at water's side
They gave me courage peace and hope
Whilst on that road I bide

The sunbeams on the foliage
The whispers on the breeze
They carried me in solace
Although my heart would freeze

So fear not your troubles
They never seem so bad
Let Mother Nature cradle you

And make you feel glad

The doe that roams the woodlands
The damselfly above the stream
The firefly in the twilight
Delivering her gentle gleam

They all are free of anguish
They all live lives quite free
They all know where they are headed
Quite unlike you and me

Do not let your fears
Destroy your lifelong plan
Acknowledge that they do exist
But need not cause you pain

You will find all your answers
It may not be right away
But take your lead from nature
To find the straight and narrow way.

The Sun

The solar orb completes me now
Bathed in his nurturing rays
I live for the time when
His beams dispel the Winter's haze

He loves me deep
His warm caress does leave my body blessed
And when he quits the dusky sky
I yield to tender rest

This golden sphere I so adore
Sustains me through my whole
His gilded smile greets me now
Whenever I open my door

If he should leave me for a while
I know that he'll return
For my gilt-borne lord is Helios
Creator of the Dawn.

The Time That I Turned Grey

The night I learnt of aged ills
Discomfort, fear and pain
The day I heard of my parents' frailty
Was the day that I turned grey.

The night my love lost motherhood
Children never to be born
The day her blood turned to solid form
Was the day that I turned grey

The night my eldest spread his wings
And left for pastures new
The time another's skin rebelled poisoned by solar rays

And then their father's did the same
Was the day that I turned grey

The hour my car was torn apart
Whilst racing on the track
It spun me on into the chicane
I ended on my back

I should have left that awful place
Encased in walls of pine
But although that night my hair turned grey
I did not go flat-line

The time that those I thought of highly

Turned their backs on me
They favoured others much more slyly
Pressuring me upon my way

They forced my hand, they made me pay
Then I left their harsh society
The very day that happened
Was the day that I turned grey

The night my closest friend on earth
made a very grave mistake
then paid long and very dearly
for the direction they chose to take

For the route this person had chosen
affected some few precious lives
Not only hurting one good soul
but several who could no longer thrive

Because he wasn't the man I thought I knew
Our friendship could not sustain
Because he ripped through other dreams
That night my hair went grey

Although my life has had its hurts
Trials and travails
At least I live to tell the tale
About the time that I turned grey.

The Written Word; Unwritten

I need to tell you something
Though' I can't quite spell it out
Maybe if I wrote it
It could more easily come out

My head is full of questions
All vying for response
I feel like I don't know you
And never did even once

I don't think you could tell me
Quite what I need to hear
If only I could write it
I don't know if it would come near.

But then maybe I am completely wrong
One half of your same whole
Maybe I shouldn't be other where
Living life on my own

The gap that leaves
One cannot tell
Although I might well grieve
But then maybe that I should quell
Perhaps they do deceive

Who knows just on what road the future lies
Fueled by love or greed

It matters not in very truth
For it is by fate decreed

It matters not what life you've lead
Or what future life you'll lead
Because when you see the bottom line
If you are cut you bleed

So let us live our lives unhurt
Uncursed by word unwritten
Let us live and let us talk
Never by cloying silence smitten

If I could say just what I feel
Tell you what I mean
Then this poem would never be….
The written word; unwritten.

These Foreign Fields

(For Owen)

Yes I have trodden those foreign fields
Where long ago had war begun
Seen the reddened poppies peaceful
Despite the battle's rising hum

As I ambled through the village of Tricourt
Or through Arras's town square
I almost heard the shellfire
And saw trenchant cannon's flare

In Picardy I walked the lines
Of trenches long since buried
And there heard low moans of despair
Of soldiers from the D Day beaches ferried

I smelt the cigarette smoke
I watched the Ypres stretcher bearers go
Out to retrieve the too soon fallen
Though it happened long ago

Loretto Heights and Vimy Ridge
Aisne Marne and Champagne too
I speak the truth I roamed them all
Not heeding what was true

Then I came down to the banks

of the ravaged River Somme
still strewn with bodies ripped and torn
youth destroyed and life long gone

In the evening sun – a blast racked tree
Stood strewn with flesh and blood
And the blood dripped down through the branches
To a corpse limbless, face down in the mud

As I stood there in solitude
At the river's side – a breeze
Reprised the rattle of the guns
And brought me to my knees

Such horror and such carnage
Was hard to take indeed
As the rusty river ran with blood
Fed by cruel harvest of the country's seed

I shall never leave the River Somme
Here remains my destiny you see
For I was the owner of that limbless corpse
Lain beneath the blast racked tree

So now, as my spirit lingers here
One of the fallen of that war
I beg of you remember us
Even though we are no more

Yes I am still in that foreign field
And was when war began
Seeing the poppies swaying – so peaceful
Despite the battle's fearful hum.

To the Moon

The Moon – the Moon is rising
Her pale orb aloft
Above the earth's shy darkness
Reflecting light so soft

I wish the moon was living
Not made from pallid stone
Then she could descend
Down from the heights
To grace an earthly throne

I wonder at the dreams
The stories she could tell
The vistas of true paradise
Of purgatory and hell

Although the moon is lonely
Up in her celestial tower
She cannot grieve to be apart
From all the races lower

The scenes that she might see
We could not even glean
The horror of war, famine and dispute
The movement of the seas

If I could visit with the moon
Radiant in all her beauty

I know that she without a doubt
would rule with constancy in duty

If I could dwell away from earth
I would hire me to the heavens
To live with her my lunar liege
In deepest peace unleavened.

Where Shadows Fear to Tread

The clouds of night are closing in
The mists are gathering round
The silence is uneasy here
Where shadows fear to tread

Old evil roams around these parts
Eager to do harm
Instilling fear in honest hearts
hailing Lucifer to arms

This cave of hell; this den of vice
A nest of vipers is
A deadly angel's harbored there
Where shadows fear to tread

The fallen one whose home it is
Has spirits at his command
And from this place at dead of night
They start to roam the land

The shades of evil murderers
The rapists of the true
The beasts of pure depravity
That righteous people slew

Here remains their haven
Just where they lay their head
While plotting dire torment

All from a fiery bed

Satan knows his servants
He knows they serve him well
Whether on this astral plane
Or further down… in hell.

Beelzebub calls them this night
Prepared to do his bidding
They gather round him thick and fast
To see the ferment brewing

For this night they will seal the curse
They'll make the nightmare happen
For 'tis the night of all the saints
When all honest folk are napping
They spread dissent they spread disease
Sarcophagi they open
Tonight they release the dead to walk again
Spreading torment and whispers of ill omen

Not only in this lair of sin
Does this pestilence persist
But also in the hearts of men
That read the devil's list

Those that have no scruples
That live life on a whim
Taking the good lord's name in vain
Perpetuating sin

For like the demonic servants
These beings have no soul

They have no care for others
Chaos their only goal

Where shadows fear to tread
They go; welcoming the archfiend's host
Then stray down other paths, to spread despair
A purgatory of ghosts.
Where shadows fear to tread they wait
To trap the lost unwary
Then taunt them with infernal hate
Leaving them with malice staring

Not only do they spread the ague
Of madness, fear and untamed fury
They seek to swell their vile clans
In the name of Belial's glory

The adversary will draw them in
These poor and tempted souls
He'll drag them down deep down and down
Into the darkest pits

They shall not see the earth again
Not as good Christians are
Their real nature's full destroyed
Their essence wholly corrupted

No one can help these poor lost souls
They are beyond retrieval
Consumed by anger, fury and hate
Prisoners of evil

The dark winged angel holds them long

Instilling all his dreadful powers
Then releases them to tread the earth again
To haunt old isolated towers

He hurts them hard
He pricks their thoughts
He rips their beings to shreds
Before he sends them on closer to
The populace to get inside their heads.

Those strong in faith
Might just withstand those trials
That are soon to come
While hope survives and faith prevails
The right things will be done

Those who walk in the ways of the Lord
Those who turn the other cheek
The righteous, generous, bold and brave
The gentle, poor and meek

Would you be in that gathering?
Or goodness do you dread?
Paving your own way to Hell
Where Shadows fear to tread.

Winter Dreams

White snow lies upon the ground
And icicles are hanging
While milkmen run their rounds
Postmen letter boxes banging

I lie dreaming in my bed
Of chestnuts hot and roasting
Of children out with apple cheeks
Of snowmen built a-boasting

I dream of bells on tinkling sleighs
Reindeer with noses red
I dream of yuletide festive cheer
While snoozing in my bed

In other reveries see happy scenes
Crowds skate on a frozen lake
Children write up their Christmas lists
Before the Christmas break

Christmas trees I visualise
With baubles glinting bright
A bulging Santa's sack of gifts
Travelling the world on Saint Nick's night

I wonder though, do other folks
Fare so well in dream time's lee
I fear that this won't be the case

Not all have a life like me

For some will dream of loneliness
Of poverty and need
Some will see only injury and evil times
Their masters pay no heed

Some will dream of hopeless violence
Of family they have lost
Many will see hunger –
Food has too high a cost

So let us not forget those souls
Help them learn to cope
Give them at least at Christmas
The possibility of hope.